THE NOVELTY OF GREEK CUISINE

MW00666930

Νικόλας Πουλμεντης

28 July 1929 — 28 February 2013

This book is for my late father, Nikolas Poulmentis, to whom I owe my life.

Thank you for always sharing your world with me, for letting me be your assistant fisherman when I was only five-years-old, and, most of all, for pushing me to pursue my dream of becoming a chef.

Copyright © 2021 Nicholas Poulmentis

All rights reserved. No part of this publication may be reproduced, distributed, or transmitted in any form or by any means, including photo-copying, recording, or other electronic or mechanical methods, without the prior written permission of the publisher or author, except in the case of brief quotations embodied in critical reviews and certain other noncommercial uses permitted by copyright law.

Recipe photography by Ilir Rizaj
Book design by Athena M. Villard

ISBN 978-1-09837-442-6

For copyright permission requests, email Villanelle Press with subject line "Attention: Copyright Permissions" at the address below.

For information about special discounts for bulk purchases, please contact Villanelle Press at the email listed below.

Published by Villanelle Press
www.villanellepress.com
Contact: villanelle@athenavillard.com

THE NOVELTY
OF
GREEK CUISINE

CHEF NICHOLAS POULMENTIS

Recipe Photography by Ilir Rizaj

Villanelle Press

CONTENTS

INTRODUCTION

Welcome to The Novelty of Greek Cuisine

I'm Chef Nicholas Poulmentis. I am an Executive Chef based in New York City and am originally from Kythira, Greece. This is my first ever cookbook, so I have chosen to share the story of what led me to where I am today as a Chef, starting on Kythira and ending with the present.

Γεια μας!
(Cheers!)

Early Years on Kythira

I found my love of food in Kythira, the island I grew up on in the Peloponnese region of Greece. It was on this most abundant island that I learned to fish, hunt, and forage. When I was a child, my father would bring me to the harbor to dive in the shallows for fish that we could bring home to our family for dinner that evening. We would catch whatever swam beneath the water's surface during that particular season. Together we could catch wild octopus, branzino, langoustine (karavida), pandora fish (lithrini), and pink snapper (fagri), to name a few.

Kythira is an exceptionally abundant island because of its varied terrains. Besides its surrounding waters, the island also possesses mountains and plenty of room for wild herbs, grapevines, and trees—most notably bearing olives, pears, figs, and legumes—throughout. I couldn't stop myself from scavenging for fresh ingredients; often taking the long way home from the harbor. On my hunt for new flavors I could combine with that day's catch, I'd sometimes collect anise and thyme from the side of the road, while other times I'd pick some of my favorite wild grapes, Petrolanos, to make home-made white wine. I'll never forget the distinctly dry flavor of that wine, which was unique to my island. During summer, I would always use it when cooking/grilling a freshly caught octopus for my friends by the beach.

This recurring cookout soon expanded into a weekly tradition including my friends, my family, and sometimes even other locals. Everyone looked forward to tasting the next creation, never the same but always prepared with local ingredients. Looking back, it's clear that my culinary passion in Kythira sprouted from these two things: first, that my cooking brought people together; and second, that I could take classic, local resources and create something unique, all the while preserving the love and respect that other people on the island had for them.

For My Father

When I was about five-years-old, my father was my hero; I wanted nothing more than to be just like him. So, when he'd take his boat out for the day, I'd beg him to let me be his assistant. He finally brought me fishing with him on his boat for the first time. He sailed us out until we cleared the shallow waters and prepared to fish. Afraid that I might fall into the sea, he dressed me in a life jacket and fastened a rope between it and the boat's mast. This was a hilarious sight to behold: a five-year-old me, practically leashed in place and, nevertheless, determined to imitate his every move as he adjusted the boat's sails.

As I grew older, my father would take me diving for octopus in the harbor's shallow waters. We couldn't use hooks to catch them because they could easily evade them or remove the hook on their own, so my father taught me to catch them by hand. There wasn't much to it except trial and error. Sometimes I would dive to catch one and they would escape with ease or spew ink, but by the end of the afternoon, I had caught one of my own. My father then taught me how to prepare the octopus for the grill and a few other tricks of the trade. I learned that, in order to wring out the excess water within the octopus, I had to hit it on a smooth rock between 100 and 150 times. After that, I would lay the octopus out in the sun to dry out some more. My father explained this is because the octopus, like any other living being, is mostly made up of water, and if I had grilled it without this preparation, then the octopus would have felt like a rubber ball.

On both these occasions, my father had immersed me into his world of centuries-old Greek traditions, and without realizing it, indoctrinated me into a lifelong passion for seafood that would quickly expand into a love of cooking.

My father always wanted me to be a doctor or an athlete. But when he saw how deep my passion for food was and how much I loved sharing that passion with everyone around me, he let go of his dreams and helped make mine come true. Without telling me, he applied to a culinary school in Greece for me when I finished high school at 17-years-old. When he received my acceptance letter, he proceeded to enroll me and surprise me with the news, telling me to always follow my heart.

Time Away From Kythira

When I finished culinary school in Greece, I applied to *Le Cordon Bleu* culinary school in Paris, France so that I could learn more about classic French cuisine and fine dining. The skills I learned at *Le Cordon Bleu* in tandem with those learned from my upbringing in Kythira and school in Greece gave me a greater command of my gastronomical knowledge and how to apply it to enhance the traditional Greek cuisine I grew up with. I had already evolved so much as an aspiring chef by this point, but I felt it was time for me to step into a professional kitchen.

When my time in Paris came to a close, I applied for a 3-month contract with a Swiss chef named Helen Zwisard, who showed me what it really means to be a chef. Chef Zwisard inspired me to refine and modernize my traditional Greek cooking by instilling two principles in me: first, that I must always hold on to and embrace my native traditions and cuisine; and second, that I must always aim to breathe new life into those same traditions and cuisines.

Returning to Kythira

When I returned home after culinary school and working in Switzerland for three months, my father smiled big and almost immediately handed me the keys to Cengo, our family hotel's restaurant and said, "it's all yours, do what you want with it."

At Cengo, I worked on incorporating different techniques and skills from all styles of European cooking in order to elevate Kythirian Greek cuisine. While my new goal was to grow and evolve my culinary expertise, I never stopped seeing myself as a fundamentally Greek chef and always felt that Kythira was my home. The experience of returning home to pursue my dream in my own family's restaurant was an honor, and all the traditions I started as a teenager officially had a venue of their own.

One of my favorite of these traditions was my Annual Easter Lamb Roast:

> Every year on Easter morning, I would wake up at 4am to go to the beach and cook 4 lambs on spits. By the time everyone left church after Easter service, the lambs would be ready for everyone to eat. I treasured this yearly event because at least 200 people would come to spend the rest of their day together over a simple, traditional meal on the beach. Bringing people together has always been my most cherished side-effect of good cooking. Traditions like these are what made me feel like I was giving back to my community, giving everyone a reason to be together as an island-wide family.

For 19 years, I ran Cengo and loved it. Having been so well acquainted with the terrain and perpetually immersed in the daily search for new flavors around the island, running this restaurant felt like I was still that same boy who, at 15, would meet with his friends weekly to sit around a fire, using large stones as plates for the fish he had grilled for everyone. I grilled fish for them on a weekly basis, always ready with a new idea to hear their opinions about. This part of me didn't change before I owned Cengo, and it still hasn't ever since.

Moving To New York City

When Greece's economy collapsed, I moved with my wife and two-year-old daughter to build my career in New York City. Within a few months of living in New York, I was selected to be a guest chef at the White House during the week of Greek Independence Day. This opportunity was so incredible for me as beforehand I felt like I was starting my career all over again in the US and it gave me a glimpse of what I could one day achieve here.

In New York, I took on a position as Head Chef at Kellari Taverna, a traditional Greek restaurant in midtown. This is where I had my first taste of success as a chef in New York City. I breathed new life into the classic Greek mezze dish Tarama Salata, dubbing it the Black Tarama (as seen on the book's cover). See page 20 for the full story and recipe! This is also where I met two great friends of mine—Chef Jean-Christophe Villard, who was the General Manager at the time, and Ilir Rizaj, who is the talented photographer behind this book. Jean-Christophe taught me the dynamics of the vast and competitive NYC culinary scene. He helped me to see that I could make a name for myself here, and I did.

After Kellari Taverna, I became the head chef at Theo's on the upper east side of New York until it closed. It was because of my exposure there that I was offered the chance to be cast for the Food Network's competitive show *Chopped*. I ended up winning the competition and was later featured on *Chopped Champions* as well as a few other Food Network shows. Since then, I've moved on to open my own restaurant, where I have truly been able to spread my wings as a Chef. At this stage of my life, I have developed and redeveloped recipes I am very proud of, many of which are featured in this book. They are **The Novelty of Greek Cuisine**.

With this book, I aim to pay homage to my roots while also sharing my evolution, both as a chef and as a person. I hope you enjoy seeing into my most treasured memories and, most of all, that they bring you as much joy as they have for me.

APPETIZERS + MEZZE

You might recognize this recipe from the front cover of the book. It is perhaps the star recipe in this collection, and for good reason. This recipe is special to me; it captures both my essence as a chef, and my first taste of success in New York City.

My cooking is predominantly based around my love of seafood. I try my best to bring flavors together from the bottom of the sea to the beautiful sunny shallows. This dish captures those unique textures and flavours that Greek seafood has to offer: black and salty squid ink, and the rich, creamy, smokiness of tarama. One ingredient from the shallows, and another from the deep.

I first unified these ingredients at a restaurant in New York, where I would serve an octopus ink pasta as well as a traditional tarama salata. The tarama salata dish progressed as I did: I eventually turned it into a mousse and, inspired by my octopus ink pasta, thought to myself, "what if I take this already non-traditional dish of tarama salata mousse and infuse it with squid ink?" This elevated both its appearance and taste, giving the tarama depth with an earthy flavor. It was a good plate, but it was missing something. One day, I decided to replace the olive oil with truffle oil to make it that little bit more decadent, and this was the exact change the recipe needed to amplify it. You'll see me mention this addition in the tips at the end of the recipe. Try it, you won't be disappointed.

After all these alterations, the recipe that I was left with, whilst true to its core, was nothing like the original Greek classic that it evolved from. I wasn't sure what people would think after all these changes to such a classic recipe, but watching their faces light up at the very first bite was all the confirmation that I needed as a chef starting out in a big city like New York.

Black Tarama

10 Servings

INGREDIENTS

Black Tarama

1 ½ cups White Tarama or Raw Herring Eggs (188g)

1 ½ cups Fresh Lemon Juice (355mL)

½ Red Onion

2 cups Vegetable Oil (475mL)

2 ½ tbsp Cuttlefish Ink

16-18 slices Soft White Bread (2in/5cm thick)

Coral Tuile

2 ½ tsp All-Purpose Flour

1 tsp Squid Ink

⅓ cup Water (80mL)

7 oz Vegetable Oil (220mL)

1 tbsp Extra Virgin Olive Oil

PREPARATION

Black Tarama

1. Dice the onion, then add to a food processor, add the lemon juice, tarama, and cuttlefish ink. Blend until fully combined.

2. Add one slice of bread to the food processor and blend until combined. Repeat this step until there is no bread left and the mixture is fully incorporated. It should have a creamy consistency.

3. Then, while the food processor is running, slowly pour in the vegetable oil with a continuous and thin stream, allowing the mixture to emulsify and thicken. Set aside.

Coral Tuile & Assembly

1. Add all of the ingredients EXCEPT olive oil to a squeeze bottle and shake thoroughly until fully combined.

2. Set a saucepan over medium heat, and add 1 tbsp extra virgin olive oil. Once the oil begins to sizzle, squeeze ~2 tbsp of the tuile mixture into the pan. Let this sizzle until you see small holes forming. When these holes form, remove the tuile from the pan using a spatula and set it onto parchment paper to dry.

3. Repeat step 2 until out of squid ink mixture. Then, serve black tarama over top of coral tuile. Enjoy.

TIP *Instead of vegetable oil, I highly recommend using truffle oil to give this an added richness.*

Dakos for Two

2-4 Servings

INGREDIENTS

Dakos

2.2 lbs Carob Rusk (1kg)

7 tbsp Butter, melted (100g)

Greek Salad Topping

1 Tomato

½ Medium Cucumber

¼ cup Kalamata Olives (90g)

1 oz Feta Cheese (25g)

1 tbsp Capers

2 tbsp Extra Virgin Olive Oil

Salt, to taste

Oregano, to taste

Black Pepper, to taste

This recipe can be made with many different kinds of rusk, but carob rusk gives a kick to your palate unlike any other! ***You will need*** *2-4 cooking rings or ramekins. These should be approximately 3-inches in diameter and be at least 3-inches deep. If you only have smaller ones, you may a few mini dakos. If you only have bigger ones, you may have one for all to share.*

PREPARATION

1. Dice the tomato and the cucumber, then roughly chop the olives. Combine all of the Greek salad ingredients in a bowl. Mix well and set aside.

2. Transfer carob rusks into a food processor and pulse until finely ground. Add the melted butter and pulse until combined.

3. Grease two cooking rings with oil and place each of them on a plate. If you do not have cooking rings, grease two ramekins. Transfer the rusk mixture into each ring or ramekin until 2-inches high. Compress the rusk using a glass or a compression tool and refrigerate for at least 15 minutes. Then, remove from the fridge.

4. **If using cooking rings,** top the compressed rusks with the greek salad mixture until the ring is completely filled. Refrigerate this for another 15 minutes. Then, once time is up, remove the rings.

   If using ramekins, cover each one with a plate and flip it so that the ramekin is upside down on top of the plate. Tap the ramekins with a spoon a few times to help the rusk release and remove the ramekins to reveal the rusk. Top the rusk with the greek salad mixture. Serve and enjoy!

Fakes Keftedes

12 Servings

INGREDIENTS

1 cup Red Lentils (190g)

1 cup Golden Bulgur Wheat (182g)

2 Scallions

2 Garlic Cloves

1 bunch of Parsley

2 tbsp Tomato Paste

1 tsp Cumin

2 tsp Salt

1 tbsp Extra Virgin Olive Oil

12 Romaine Lettuce Leaves

"Fakes" means lentil & "keftedes" means meatball.
This meatless recipe is a light and refreshing appetizer for any occasion!
***NOTE** be generous with step 6! Lemon juice makes a world of a difference in this recipe.*

PREPARATION

1. Finely chop the scallions and parsley, then mince the garlic, set aside.
2. Bring water to a boil in a small to medium saucepan, add lentils and cook until al dente, approximately 5-6 minutes. Drain the lentils and rinse them with cold water to stop the cooking process. Set the drained lentils aside in a heat-safe bowl to cool.
3. In another saucepan, add 2 cups of water, bring to a boil. Then, set aside and add the golden bulgur wheat and cover until completely absorbed.
4. In a large mixing bowl, thoroughly combine the lentils, bulgur wheat, scallions, garlic, parsley, tomato paste, cumin, salt, and extra virgin olive oil.
5. Measure out 2 tbsp chunks of the mixture and roll into balls. Make a wrap with one romaine leaf and place the keftedes inside. Repeat with remaining keftedes and leaves.
6. Finish with a generous squeeze of fresh lemon juice. Serve and enjoy!

Black Garlic Tzatziki Dip

20 Servings

INGREDIENTS

1½ cups English Cucumber (180g)

2 tbsp Salt

½ gallon Greek Yogurt, thick (2.5kg)

3½ tbsp Black Garlic, puréed

3.5 fl oz Extra Virgin Olive Oil (100mL)

¼ cup Moscatel vinegar (59mL)

3 tbsp Dill

½ tsp White Pepper

This is not your average tzatziki!
It's a signature recipe of mine and I make it often. Black garlic is very underrated and adds a depth of flavor to this classic tzatziki that I know you'll enjoy!

PREPARATION

1. **One day ahead,** shred the english hothouse cucumber using the largest side of a common cheese grater. Place the cucumber shreddings into a perforated bowl. Season very generously with salt and set over another bowl.

2. Add all of the ingredients EXCEPT for the cucumber and dill into a stand mixer with a hook attachment. Mix on medium-low speed for 12-15 minutes.

3. Finely chop the dill, then add to the mixer with the cucumber. Mix on medium-low speed again for another 5 minutes.

4. Refrigerate overnight and the tzatziki will be ready the next day.

5. Serve with some extra virgin olive oil drizzled over top and enjoy!

TIP *If you would like a tzatziki with a stronger taste of fennel, then try these minor changes to the recipe: Instead of black garlic, use 2 tbsp of minced white garlic and cure the shredded cucumber in ouzo.*

Stuffed Zucchini Blossoms

12 Servings

INGREDIENTS

12 Zucchini Blossoms

2 cups Israeli Couscous or Quinoa (360g)

1 Tomato

1 Green Bell Pepper

1 Onion

2 tbsp Dill

2 Garlic Cloves

½ bunch Parsley

4 oz Feta Cheese, crumbled (100g)

~24 Fresh Mint Leaves

1 tbsp Salt

1 tsp Black Pepper

34 fl oz Chicken Stock (1 L)

2 cups Greek Yogurt (570g)

This is a seasonal recipe since zucchini blossoms are only available in summer.

PREPARATION

1. Add quinoa/couscous to a pot of boiling water and cook for 12 minutes. Strain thoroughly and set aside to cool.

2. Dice the tomato, green bell pepper, and onion into small cubes. Then, finely chop the dill, garlic, parsley, and fresh mint. Add to the quinoa with crumbled feta, salt, and pepper. Combine.

3. Gently stuff the mixture into each zucchini blossom using a small spoon until the blossom is almost full.

4. Place zucchini blossoms in a pot and pour chicken stock into the pot until only the bottom half of the blossoms are submerged. Cover and simmer for 15 minutes.

5. Serve with greek yogurt and drizzle extra virgin olive oil over top. Enjoy!

Shrimp Loukoumades

4 Servings

INGREDIENTS

Shrimp

20 Jumbo Shrimp, (size 21/25)

1 tsp Black Sesame Seeds

1 tsp White Sesame Seeds

Sambal Aioli (Spicy)

2 qt Mayonnaise (1.6kg)

¾ cup Sambal Paste (180g)

2 tbsp Soy Sauce

2 tbsp Dry Ginger Powder

2 tbsp Fish Sauce

4 tbsp Sesame Oil

Gluten-Free Tempura

1 cup Rice Flour (160g)

¾ cup Beer, *blonde recommended* (180mL)

2-3 cups Vegetable Oil (450-700mL)

You will need *a frying/candy thermometer for this recipe.*

PREPARATION

1. Add all aioli ingredients into a food processor and pulse until well combined, set aside.

2. **Prep the shrimp,** trim away the head and peel each shrimp, making sure to remove the vein from the underside of each shrimp as well. Set aside.

3. Mix the tempura ingredients (beer and rice flour) together until a thick paste forms, set aside.

4. Fill a large saucepan with vegetable oil until it's at least two inches deep and bring to 375°F (190°C). Meanwhile, cut each shrimp into 3 pieces and coat them all with the tempura mixture.

5. One at a time, submerge and fry the coated shrimps in the oil until they are golden brown.

6. Transfer the fried shrimp into a large bowl and toss with 2 tbsp of sambal aioli, and the black and white sesame seeds until nicely coated.

7. Serve with extra sambal aioli and enjoy!

Jarred Fouskes

5 Servings

INGREDIENTS

Fouskes

10-20 Fouskes Oysters

1 tsp Extra Virgin Olive Oil

Brine

7 parts Filtered Water

1 part Sea Salt

Fouska is a type of soft-shelled oyster that only lives off the coast of Greece. This recipe makes a delicious savory snack. ***You will need*** *an 8 oz-sized heat-safe jar.*

PREPARATION

1. To prepare the jar(s) for the fouskes and brine, they must be sterilized. Wash and dry jars, then place in a 300°F (150°C) oven for 30 minutes to sanitize. Once time is up, remove jars from the oven and allow to cool.

2. To prepare the brine, combine 7 parts water to 1 part sea salt and mix until salt is completely dissolved, set aside.

3. Cut the fouskes' soft shells in half and, using a spoon, scoop the oysters out of their shells and transfer to the cooled sterile jar until it is full, about 15 fouskes.

4. Pour the brine over the oysters until covered and add the extra virgin olive oil. Close the jar tightly and set upside down for 4 hours before transferring to the refrigerator. Enjoy!

Grilled Artichokes

6 Servings

INGREDIENTS

16 Whole Artichokes

5 tbsp Extra Virgin Olive Oil (approx.)

Sea Salt, to taste

Lemon Juice, to taste

PREPARATION

1. Trim away artichoke stems and discard.Roll each artichoke on your work surface in order to soften, then place the artichokes side by side on a baking tray and season with extra virgin olive oil and sea salt.

2. **If you are using the oven**, preheat it to 375°F (190°C). Place artichokes on the top rack of the oven and bake for 30-35 minutes until nicely charred. **If you are using the grill,** set seasoned artichokes on charcoal grill and cover. Allow to cook for 30-35 minutes until nicely charred.

3. When ready, remove from the oven/grill and season with extra virgin olive oil once more. One by one, peel away the artichoke leaves until only the heart is left.

4. Cut away the choke (looks hairy) and season the heart with 5 tbsp extra virgin olive oil, lemon juice, and sea salt. Serve and enjoy!

Charcoal Vlita

4-6 Servings

A member of the amaranth greens family, vlita is a staple of the Greek diet because of its abundant nutritional value as well as its mild flavor. My parents used to grow vlita in our garden on Kythira. A few years ago, I brought some seeds from my family garden on Kythira back to New York in hopes of growing it here. The wonderful people at 1760 Homestead Farm in Northville, NY cultivated my seeds into the same beautiful vlita that I grew up eating.

INGREDIENTS

3 lbs Vlita (1.4kg)

12 cups Water (3L)

2 tbsp Sea Salt

Extra Virgin Olive Oil, to taste

Red Wine Vinegar, to taste

PREPARATION

1. Take a large pot and set over a charcoal fire. Add water and bring to a boil. Then, add vlita to the pot. Cook for 7-9 minutes, stirring occasionally.

2. Discard all liquid and serve immediately with extra virgin olive oil, sea salt, and red wine vinegar. Enjoy!

Raw Tuna with Eggplant Purée & Lime Caviar

4-6 Servings

INGREDIENTS

Eggplant Purée

2 Eggplants

1 Garlic Clove

3 tbsp White Vinegar

1 tsp Salt

½ tsp Black Pepper

1 cup Vegetable Oil (237mL)

Tuna

8 oz Raw Tuna (226g)

2 Finger Limes

1 tsp Black Sesame Seeds

½ tbsp Sesame Oil

½ Avocado

While the raw tuna and eggplant purée may be the main elements of this dish, the finger limes very easily steal the spotlight. These may not be available at your average market, but I strongly suggest seeking them out to experience the tiny citrus pearls pop in your mouth. Be sure that your raw tuna is freshly caught and/or sushi-grade!

PREPARATION

Eggplant Purée

1. Poke eggplants all over to create small holes for steam to escape while grilling. Grill eggplants until fully caramelized, about 17-20 minutes, flipping every 5 minutes.

2. Remove the eggplant skins and cut into medium sized chunks. Transfer the chopped eggplant into a blender or food processor with garlic, vinegar, salt, and pepper. Blend on high speed until well incorporated.

3. With the blender still running, slowly pour in the vegetable oil with a continuous and thin stream, allowing the mixture to emulsify and thicken. Set aside the purée.

Tuna & Assembly

1. Dice avocado and set into a medium mixing bowl. Then, cut each finger lime in half crosswise and empty contents into the same bowl, reserving some to the side for garnish.

2. Dice the tuna into cubes and transfer to the mixing bowl which already contains the avocado and lime caviar. Add in sesame seeds and sesame oil then gently mix together until lightly incorporated.

3. Plate this mixture with the eggplant purée on the side. Garnish with lime caviar and cilantro, if desired. Serve and enjoy!

Shrimp Kataifi with Yogurt Parsley Sauce

4 Servings

INGREDIENTS

Yogurt Parsley Sauce

½ cup Extra Virgin Olive Oil (118mL)
3 cups Greek Yogurt, thick (855g)
1 tsp White Vinegar
3 Garlic Cloves
3 tbsp Soft Yellow Mustard
2 tbsp Sugar
3 tbsp Parsley
½ cup Scallion (50g)
1 tbsp Capers
2 ½ tbsp Salt
1 tbsp Black Pepper
¼ cup Lemon Juice (59mL)

Shrimp Kataifi

4 pieces U4 Prawns
12.3 oz Kataifi Phyllo Dough, thawed (350g)
1 ⅓ cup Butter, melted (300g)
½ cup Garlic (120g)
1 tsp Black Sesame Seeds, toasted
1 tsp White Sesame Seeds, toasted
1 tsp Salt
1 tsp Black Pepper
1 tsp Smoked Paprika
4 tbsp Parsley
4 Skewers, 12-inches long

PREPARATION

Yogurt Parsley Sauce

1. Chop the parsley, garlic, and scallion. Then add all ingredients EXCEPT extra virgin olive oil and lemon juice into a food processor. Pulse until well incorporated.

2. Then, slowly pour the extra virgin olive oil in a continuous and thin stream into the food processor while it's running. This allows the oil to emulsify into the sauce. Add the lemon juice and pulse until the sauce is medium to thick in consistency. Set aside.

Shrimp Kataifi & Assembly

1. Preheat oven to 350°F (177°C). Prep the shrimp: trim away the head and peel each shrimp, making sure to remove the vein from the underside of each shrimp as well.

2. In a bowl, mix 1 cup (225g) warm melted butter with the parsley, salt, paprika, garlic, and pepper until thoroughly incorporated. Next, add raw shrimp to the mixture and set aside to marinate at room temperature.

3. Unfold kataifi dough horizontally on a clean work surface. Separate the strands into 4 equal groups and generously brush the kataifi with remaining melted butter.

4. Skewer each shrimp from the tail up and stop short of the head so that the shrimp is straightened out along it. Wrap the kataifi dough around each one. Be sure the dough is wrapped tightly around the shrimp as it can easily unwrap itself.

5. Sprinkle the black and white sesame seeds over each shrimp and bake for 12 minutes until kataifi is golden brown. Serve and enjoy with the yogurt dipping sauce.

Crushed Potatoes with Kefalograviera

4 Servings

INGREDIENTS

4 lbs Idaho Potatoes (1.8kg)

2 cups Warm Water (475mL)

1 tbsp Chicken Base

1 tbsp Salt

1 tbsp Black Pepper

1 sprig Fresh Thyme

1 sprig Fresh Rosemary

1 lb Ground Kefalograviera (453g)

This is a 3-day ordeal, but it doesn't require much work I promise! Kefalograviera, a traditional Greek cheese, is very salty and pairs perfectly with potatoes. ***You will need*** *a frying/candy thermometer for this recipe.*

PREPARATION

Day 1

1. Preheat oven to 400°F (204°C). Cut each potato lengthwise into 4 pieces, then place in a hotel pan or large, deep baking pan and set aside.
2. Dissolve chicken base in warm water with salt and pepper. Add this mixture to the hotel pan with the potatoes. Then, add the sprigs of thyme and rosemary to the pan as well.
3. Cover the hotel pan with parchment paper, then again with aluminum foil and bake in the oven for approximately 35-40 minutes.
4. Once time is up, pull the potatoes out of the oven. Poke them to ensure that they are cooked thoroughly. Drain the liquid and remove the sprigs of rosemary and thyme from the pan. Refrigerate the potatoes overnight.

Day 2

5. Place the potatoes 4 inches apart on a sheet of parchment paper and cover with another sheet of parchment paper. Crush each potato using a meat pounder or mallet. Try not to crush them any thinner than 1-inch to preserve their texture. Refrigerate overnight.

Day 3

6. Fill a large pot with vegetable oil (at least 6-inches deep) and heat to 350°F (177°C). Place potatoes in hot oil and remove when golden brown.
7. Once the potatoes are finished frying, put them in a bowl and toss with salt and pepper to taste, add kefalograviera cheese, and serve. Enjoy!

SOUPS
+
SALADS

Kakavia is a Greek fisherman's soup that is traditionally made with the leftover catch of the day. With the addition of some very roughly chopped aromatics and some olive oil drizzled in overtop, Kakavia Soup is a great way to ensure none of the catch is wasted. Traditionally, the soup is served in a deconstructed manner, with the vegetables and fish served on separate platters and the broth served in individual bowls. I love this because it gives me the chance to savor the flavor of every element in the soup and always lets me create my own perfect bite.

As a teenager, I would often go fishing near the Port of Kythira. On my walks there, I would always be taken aback by the beautiful scent of this soup. I'd follow it until I arrived at the fisherman's boat where it was being made. One of them taught me how to make it, using only the ingredients we had at our disposal on the island. They would take fish trimmings from the leftover catch of the day and mix in tomato, celery, onions, carrots, potatoes, and olive oil. What was most interesting to me though was the way this soup is cooked and consumed.

This soup is traditionally cooked in three layers within a single, large pot. The bottom layer contains all aromatics and other vegetables which are then covered with water. The top layer consists of fish which are cut down into manageable pieces and steam-cooked by the boiling water beneath them. Between these two layers lies a bed of olive tree branches. These branches may not do much in terms of flavor, but they are instrumental in creating a barrier between the top and bottom layers. This barrier is needed to prevent the fish from losing its texture in the water as well as to prevent the bones from mixing in with the rest of the soup.

I love this method of cooking soup because, as I learned it, it is designed to only serve two people since the broth is what I like to call a "pure extract" made up of oils from the fish trickling down into the liquid below in the pot. In addition, it pays homage to the Greek fishermen who, for ages, have made this soup in the dark underbellies of their boats, in constant motion due to the crashing waves just on the other side of the wooden hull.

Kakavia Soup with Olive Branches

2 Servings

INGREDIENTS

6 Olive Tree Branches (~10 inches long)

2 Lemons

1 Tomato

2 Potatoes

1 White Onion

1 Carrot

¼ cup Extra Virgin Olive Oil (59mL)

3 Celery Sticks

1lb Whiting Fish or any small fatty fish (450g)

1 Head of White Fish

PREPARATION

1. Peel and cut the potatoes, onions, and tomatoes into quarters and place into a large pot. Then, cut both the carrots and celery into equal pieces and add to the pot as well.

2. Place the olive branches atop the vegetables and add the whiting fish and fish heads, making sure that the fish and vegetables stay separated by the branches. Add water to the pot until the vegetables are covered, then add extra virgin olive oil and salt.

TIP *If you are unable to find olive branches, please use chopsticks or skewers instead.*

3. Cover the pot and set over maximum heat for approximately 20 minutes. Then, remove from heat and uncover the pot. Add lemon juice and salt to taste.

4. Separate the layers of the soup into 3 plates. Place the fish on one plate. Add extra virgin olive oil and sea salt. Place the vegetables in another plate. Add extra virgin olive oil and sea salt. Serve and enjoy!

Stuffed Onion Avgolemono

4 Servings

INGREDIENTS

Stuffed Onions

10 Vintila Onions

2.2 lbs Shrimp 36/40 (1kg)

2 Eggs

1 bunch of Dill

1 ½ cup Risotto Rice (300g)

~15 Mint Leaves

7 tbsp Extra Virgin Olive Oil (105mL)

4 cups Chicken Stock (1L)

Salt, to taste

Black Pepper, to taste

Avgolemono

6 Eggs

2 tbsp Cornstarch

6 tbsp Lemon Juice

An avgolemono, which means "egg lemon," is an umbrella term for soups and sauces made with a mixture of eggs, lemon juice, and a stock. In this case, it is your choice whether you would like to make this avgolemono a soup or a sauce. If you would prefer a sauce, use less chicken stock when combining it with the avgolemono mixture. In the case of a soup, follow the recipe as it's written.

PREPARATION

Stuffed Onions

1. Peel the skin from the onions and set in a pot with ½ gallon (2 L) of water. Bring to a boil. 20 minutes later, remove the onions from the pot and set in a cool bath of ice water to stop the cooking process.
2. Then, make a vertical cut to each onion up to its core. Remove each layer gently, and set aside.
3. Remove the shell and tail from all the shrimp and dice into small pieces. Set the diced shrimp into a mixing bowl with the eggs, risotto rice, mint, chopped dill, and oil.
4. Scoop out 1-2 tbsp of this mixture and place on one side of every leaf of onion and wrap in the onion leaf. Do this with all the onion leaves until there's no stuffing left.
5. Make a bed in the pot using the leftover onion cores (this prevents the stuffed onion from making contact with the bottom of the pot and burning).
6. Place the rest of the onions connection-side down in a pot. Cover with 4 cups chicken stock and place a round plate atop the onions so that when the stock boils, it doesn't disturb the structure of the stuffed onions. Cook for 20 minutes over medium heat.

Avgolemono & Assembly.

1. Meanwhile, in a large mixing bowl, whisk the eggs together with lemon juice and cornstarch. When the onions are done cooking in the chicken stock, remove the pot from heat and allow the stock to settle if it's boiling. Additionally, remove the plate from within the pot.
2. To temper the eggs (so they don't scramble in the soup), slowly pour 1 cup (237mL) of hot chicken stock from the pot into the mixing bowl while whisking constantly. Once it thickens and has a silk-like texture, add the tempered egg mixture back into the pot with the stock and onions. Stir gently, making sure not to disturb the onions.
3. You may serve the avgolemono as a sauce or a soup. **If you would prefer a sauce,** then place the stuffed onions in the center of a plate and pour a small amount of avgolemono over top. **If you would prefer a soup,** then serve the onions in a bowl with the avgolemono. Enjoy!

Youvarlakia Avgolemono

4-6 Servings

INGREDIENTS

Avgolemono

6 Eggs

2 tbsp Cornstarch

6 tbsp Lemon Juice

Seafood Rice Balls

10 Medium-Large Shrimp (size 36/40)

2 Eggs

1 Onion

1 Carrot

¼ cup Extra Virgin Olive Oil (59mL)

2 cups Rice (370g)

½ cup Dill (50g)

½ cup Parsley (50g)

2 tsp Salt

1 tsp Black pepper

2 oz Pink Ginger (57g)

4 cups Chicken Stock (1L)

Avgolemono means "egg lemon" and is an umbrella term for soups and sauces made with a mixture of eggs, lemon juice, and stock. In this case, it is your choice whether you would like to make this avgolemono a soup or a sauce. If you would prefer a sauce, use less chicken stock when combining it with the avgolemono mixture. In the case of a soup, follow the recipe as it's written.

PREPARATION

Seafood Rice Balls

1. Cut the shrimp into small cubes and set aside. Finely dice the onion and carrot, then chop the parsley, dill, and ginger. Set aside.
2. Thoroughly rinse the uncooked rice in water and transfer into a bowl. Add all the other rice ball ingredients and mix well to combine.
3. Shape mixture into balls, about ⅓cup per rice ball.
4. Set romaine lettuce leaves on the bottom of a large pot to prevent the rice balls from burning as they cook.
5. Place the shaped rice balls inside the pot. Cover with 4 cups chicken stock and set over medium heat. Bring the stock to a boil and let it cook for another ten minutes.

Avgolemono & Assembly.

1. Meanwhile, in a large mixing bowl, whisk the eggs together with lemon juice and cornstarch. Once the rice balls are done cooking in the chicken stock, remove the pot from heat and allow the stock to settle if it's boiling.
2. To temper the eggs (so they don't scramble in the soup), slowly pour 1 cup (237mL) of hot chicken stock from the pot into the mixing bowl while whisking constantly. Once it thickens and has a silk-like texture, add the tempered egg mixture back into the pot with the stock and rice balls. Stir gently, making sure not to disturb the rice balls.
3. You may serve the avgolemono as a sauce or a soup. **If you would prefer a sauce,** then place the rice balls in the center of a plate and pour a small amount of avgolemono over top. **If you would prefer a soup,** then serve the rice balls in a bowl with the avgolemono. Enjoy!

Every time I make this recipe, I think back to when I was a teenager living on Kythira, when I would go fishing every weekend with my best friend Dennis. We would walk along the harbor together to get to our fishing spot. One of these excursions was just a week after I had gotten a new pair of white sneakers that had quickly become my favorites. I remember looking down at them and marvelling at the way they blinded me as they reflected the sunlight; seeing that I was distracted, Dennis took the opportunity to shove me into the shallow waters of the harbor.

He laughed as I yelled at him from the water. I was walking back through the shallows, towards land, when something began to wrap itself around my ankles. I looked down to find that, instead of seeing my white sneakers reflecting back at me through the clear waters, there was an octopus. I was shocked to see this since octopi don't usually roam shallow waters, especially not during the winter months. I swiftly kneeled down and snatched the octopus off my ankles and lifted it above my head for Dennis and everyone else around the harbour to see. I was the luckiest person alive. That evening, I sat down with my family and Dennis to eat this good luck charm.

This recipe will have between six and eight servings in it. This is because there is one tentacle per serving and, despite their name, the exact amount of tentacles on an octopus does vary.

Octopus & Black Eyed Pea Salad

7-8 Servings

INGREDIENTS

1 6-8 lb Octopus, pref. Mediterranean (2.7-3.6kg)

4 cups Canned Black Eyed Peas (684g)

1 ½ bunch Dill

4-5 Scallions

4-6 tbsp Moscatel Vinegar

6-8 tbsp (90-120mL) Extra Virgin Olive Oil

2 tsp Sea Salt

Oregano, to taste

PREPARATION

1. Fill a large pot with cold water, place the octopus into the pot and set over medium heat for 1 hour and 15 minutes, uncovered.

2. Meanwhile, finely chop the dill and scallions and set aside. Next, drain the canned black eyed peas and thoroughly wash then dry them. In a mixing bowl, add the black eyed peas, extra virgin olive oil, salt, scallions, dill, and vinegar. Mix well and set aside.

3. Once time is up, take the octopus out of the water and poke the octopus with a knife where the tentacle meets the head. If it pops through the skin and passes through easily, it's fully cooked. If it is not finished, then put it back over heat for 5 more minutes at most.

4. Once it is fully cooked, refrigerate it to stop the cooking process. Leave it in the fridge until it is no longer hot to the touch. Cut tentacles away from the octopus' head and set the head aside.

NOTE *We will not be using the octopus head in this recipe, but I highly recommend making octopus cakes. They are like crab cakes, but better!*

5. Grill each octopus tentacle, suction cup-side up, for 5 minutes each.

6. Serve the black eyed pea salad on 7-8 plates and place one octopus tentacle atop each salad. Finish with extra virgin olive oil and oregano, both to taste. Enjoy!

Candy Cane Beet Salad

2 Servings

INGREDIENTS

Beets

6 Large Beets, Red and/or Golden

⅓ cup Red Wine Vinegar (79mL)

½ cup Extra Virgin Olive Oil (118mL)

1 tbsp Sea Salt

Mousse

3.5 oz Feta Cheese (100g)

1.75 oz Goat Cheese (50g)

½ cup Heavy Cream (118mL)

1 tsp Black Pepper

2 tbsp Extra Virgin Olive Oil

Garnish

1 Candy Cane Beet

⅓ cup Roasted Almonds (37g)

PREPARATION

Beets

1. Preheat oven to 450°F (230°C).

2. Add the beets to a large, deep baking dish. Fill the pan with water until the beets are covered. Then, cover the pan firmly with parchment paper and aluminum foil over top. Bake this for 60 minutes until softened.

   TIP *Use a knife to check if the core is softened. DO NOT boil red and golden beets together if using both varieties, this will dye the golden ones red.*

3. When time is up, take the beets out of the oven and immediately drain the liquid from the pan. Set them aside at room temperature, allowing them to cool completely.

4. Once cooled, remove the skin from the beets using a towel and dice into small cubes. Place the diced beets into a mixing bowl with extra virgin olive oil, red vinegar, and salt. Mix thoroughly and refrigerate to marinate.

Mousse & Assembly

1. Using a mandolin with a 0.01 cm-sized blade to thinly slice the candy cane beet. If you do not have a mandolin, use a knife to slice the beet as thinly as you are able. Set aside.

2. In a food processor, add all the mousse ingredients and pulse carefully until well combined. Be careful not to overmix as it may ruin the texture of the mousse.

3. Transfer the mixture into a pastry bag and pipe the mousse onto each plate. Drain the marinade out of the diced beets and place them atop the mousse.

4. Season with roasted almonds and top with the candy cane beet slices. Serve and enjoy!

Eggplant Trahana

Servings

INGREDIENTS

1 lb Eggplant (450g)

3 cups Chicken Stock (710mL), plus extra

1 lb Trahana Cheese (450g)

1 tsp Salt

1 tsp Black Pepper

½ lb Feta, garnish (227g)

2 Fire Roasted Peppers, florinas preferred

3 tbsp Extra Virgin Olive Oil

1 ½ tbsp Red Wine Vinegar, moscatel preferred

PREPARATION

1. Dice peppers, set aside. Boil the chicken stock over medium heat. Gradually add in the trahana cheese, mixing constantly. Do not leave your pot's side as it is very easy for the trahana to stick.

NOTE *You may need to add more chicken stock as the trahana is very absorbent. If the mixture begins to look dry, slowly add more chicken stock, stirring constantly, until you reach the desired consistency. If you run out of extra chicken stock, you may use water. We are looking for softened grains and absorbed liquid.*

2. Once the desired consistency is reached, remove pot from heat and, using a fine mesh sieve, strain this mixture into a medium bowl. Leave the sieve sitting above the bowl and set aside to allow the mixture to strain fully.

3. Poke holes in the eggplants on all sides, these will act as vents to allow steam to escape as they cook. It is preferable to cook them on a smoky grill until soft and caramelized on the inside. If you cannot use a grill, preheat your oven to 375°F (191°C) and place them on baking sheets. Bake eggplants until softened, approximately 45 minutes, turning them once every 15 minutes.

4. Once softened, remove eggplants from the grill/oven and remove skin (be careful not to burn yourself!). Leave them in a colander over the sink to allow their liquid to drain. You want about 90% of the liquid to have drained from the eggplant. Afterwards, finely dice them; this will almost purée them as they will already be very soft.

5. Crumble the feta cheese and add into a large bowl with the cooked trahana, eggplant, roasted peppers, salt, black pepper, and vinegar. Serve and enjoy warm or hot.

Marouli Salata

2 Servings

INGREDIENTS

2 heads of Romaine Lettuce

3 Scallions

7 sprigs of Dill

4 tbsp Extra Virgin Olive Oil

3 tbsp Moscatel Vinegar

4 tbsp Feta Cheese (72g)

This recipe remains one of my favorites. The moscatel vinegar is what truly elevates this otherwise very simple dish into something worth making over and over again.

PREPARATION

1. Finely chop the scallions and dill, set aside into a large salad bowl. Very thinly slice romaine lettuce and add into the same bowl.

2. Into the salad bowl, add onion, extra virgin olive oil, vinegar and toss well.

3. Incorporate the crumbled feta into the salad and serve. Enjoy!

MAIN DISHES

My sous chef and I were thinking about creating a Greek sushi recipe for the menu at my restaurant some time ago. So much of Greek cuisine is centred around the sea that it seemed like a natural coming-together of cultures. Our original idea was to create a more traditional recipe, using classic sushi ingredients such as nori/seaweed. However, it was also around this time when I was working on refining my recipe for dolmadakia, otherwise known as stuffed grape leaves. I realized that it may be more interesting, and perhaps fitting, for our Greek sushi recipe to replace the nori with grape leaves.

My sous chef and I then moved on to try this idea out and essentially recreated dolmadakia in the form of sushi; larger and sliced into bite sized pieces. This iteration of the recipe made use of japanese techniques in tandem with Greek flavors and textures. But, we wanted to take it a few steps further. We then engineered this recipe to include more of a mélange of japanese flavors and textures with those of Greek cuisine; the sharpness of the pink ginger contrasting with the subtle creamy smokiness of the tarama, the salty capers blending with the soy-sauce's umami, and the toasted sesame seeds finding their perfect home amid a mixture of Mediterranean and Japanese flavours.

After some experimentation, we came to the following recipe which distinctly emulates techniques, flavors, and textures from both Japanese and Greek cuisine. This recipe uses shrimp tempura, cucumbers, roasted red peppers, and capers as the filling with a tarama emulsion and sizzled capers on top. **You will need a bamboo sushi mat to roll the sushi as well as a frying/candy thermometer for the shrimp tempura.**

This is a dish which represents my evolution as a chef, taking inspiration from both my childhood in Kythira and my adulthood in New York. I hope you love it as much as I do.

Grape Leaf Sushi

6 Servings

INGREDIENTS

Assembly (Grape Leaves)

40 Grape leaves

1 Lemon

Sushi Rice

3 cups Sushi Rice (540g)

4 cups Water (950mL)

3 cups White Vinegar (710mL)

1 ½ cups Sugar (300g)

1 tsp Salt

1 tbsp Black Sesame Seeds, toasted

1 tbsp White Sesame Seeds, toasted

3 tbsp Soy Sauce

2 tbsp Pink Ginger

Tarama Emulsion

2 tbsp Tarama (Greek cod roe)

1 ½ tbsp Lemon Juice

1 cup Vegetable Oil

Shrimp Tempura

12 Jumbo Shrimps (size 21/25)

1 cup Rice Flour (160g)

¾ cup Beer, *blonde recommended* (180mL)

2-3 cups Vegetable Oil (450-700mL)

Filling

1 Fire Roasted Pepper

½ English Cucumber, skin on

4 tbsp Capers

1 cup Vegetable Oil (237mL)

PREPARATION

Grape Leaves

1. Preheat the oven to 350°F (177°C). Very thinly slice your lemon into at least 10 slices.
2. In a large, deep baking pan, layer the grape leaves with lemon slices between each leaf and cover with water. Cover the pan with aluminum foil and place in the oven for 60 minutes.
3. Once time is up, remove from the oven, then remove foil from the pan, and transfer the leaves into ice water. When cooled, set them aside to dry.

Sushi Rice

1. Put rice and water in a medium saucepan and set over high heat. Once the water comes to a boil, bring to low heat and cover the saucepan. Leave to cook for 30 minutes.
2. Meanwhile, combine the vinegar with sugar and salt and set aside. Then, finely chop ginger and set that aside for the next step as well.
3. Transfer the cooked rice into a mixing bowl with ½ cup (118mL) of the vinegar mixture. Add toasted black sesame seeds, toasted white sesame seeds, soy sauce, and ginger. Mix thoroughly until fully incorporated, set aside to cool.

NOTE *Never refrigerate sushi rice.*

Tarama Emulsion

NOTE *it is preferable to use an electric whisk or stand mixer while adding the oil to maintain the emulsion. Additionally, if you would like this emulsion to be pink (as seen in the photo), then add a dash of red beet juice.*

1. Add Tarama and lemon juice into a bowl and whisk until smooth. Then, while continuing to whisk, slowly pour the oil into the bowl in a continuous and thin stream, allowing the mixture to emulsify.

Grape Leaf Sushi *continued*

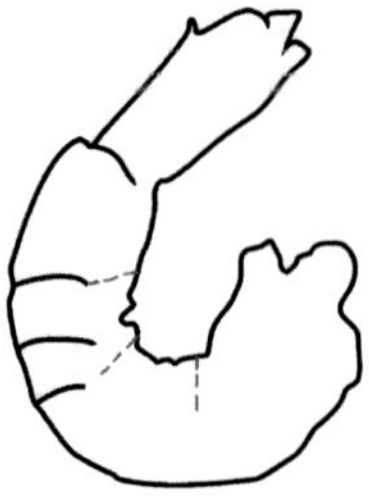

Figure 1 - Step 2

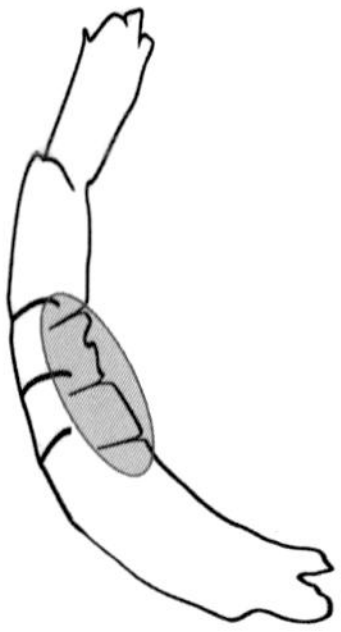

Figure 2 - Step 2

Shrimp Tempura

1. Mix the tempura ingredients (beer and rice flour) together until a thick paste forms, set aside.

2. Make about 3 shallow crosswise slices on the belly side of the shrimp in order to flatten the shrimp and create the greatest surface area possible for the tempura to coat (*see figures 1 + 2*) and to make the tempura fit in the sushi.

3. Fill a large saucepan with vegetable oil until it's at least two inches deep and bring to 375°F (190°C). One at a time, submerge and fry the coated shrimps in the oil until they are golden brown. Remove from the oil once golden brown and set over paper towels to allow the excess oil to dry away. Set aside for assembly.

Sushi Filling & Assembly

1. Fill a small saucepan with vegetable oil and bring to 350°F (177°C) on the stove. Then, gently drop in 2 tbsp of capers and allow to sizzle/fry for 1 minute before removing. Place sizzled capers over paper towels to dry well and set aside for garnish.

2. Julienne the roasted pepper and cucumber, set aside for assembly.

3. Wrap the sushi mat with plastic wrap and create a bed of grape leaves (vein side down) on top of it (*see figure* 3). Place sushi rice atop the grape leaves, spreading it out to evenly cover about two thirds of the leaves (*see figure* 4).

4. In a horizontal line, add the cucumber, roasted pepper, 2 tbsp brined capers, and 2 pieces of shrimp tempura to the center third of the bed of rice (*see figure* 5).

5. Carefully and tightly roll the sushi mat into a cylinder (*see figures* 6 & 7). Once well-rolled, remove the sushi mat & plastic wrap combo to reveal the rolled sushi.

6. Using a sharp knife, cut the roll into 8 pieces (*see figure* 8). Serve with the tarama emulsion drizzled over it and garnish with sizzled capers.

7. Repeat steps 2–6 five more times to use up all ingredients. Enjoy!

Grape Leaf Sushi *continued*

Figure 3 - Step 3

Figure 4 - Step 3

Figure 5 - Step 4

Figure 6 - Step 5

Figure 7 - Step 5

Figure 8 - Step 6

Squid Ink Pita Bread Souvlaki

8 Servings

INGREDIENTS

Squid Ink

2.2 lb Bread Flour (1kg)
¾ tbsp Apple Cider Vinegar
1.6 oz Honey (45g)
¾ tbsp Salt
1 ¾ tbsp Dry Yeast (15g)
19.4 fl oz Lukewarm Water (575mL)
2 tbsp Squid Ink

Sambal Aioli

2 qt Mayonnaise (1.6kg)
¾ cup Sambal Paste (180g)
2 tbsp Soy Sauce
2 tbsp Dry Ginger Powder
2 tbsp Fish Sauce
4 tbsp Sesame Oil

Filling

10 oz Tuna (283g)
½ tbsp Salt
1 tsp Black Pepper
1 tbsp Extra Virgin Olive Oil
6 Lettuce Leaves
½ cup Red Onion (60g)
1 Fire Roasted Pepper
1 tsp Paprika

The pita bread in this recipe has an added layer of richness to it with the squid ink while the sambal aioli slaw kicks your palate. This sandwich is all about the little details.

PREPARATION

Squid Ink Pita Bread

1. In a mixing bowl, add lukewarm water, squid ink, salt, honey, apple cider vinegar, and dry yeast. Combine these ingredients until well incorporated.
2. Slowly add the flower into the mixture, mixing well to incorporate. Once fully incorporated, the dough should no longer be sticky. Cover the bowl with plastic wrap and leave in a warm place until the dough doubles in size, at least 1 hours.
3. Once the dough has proved, remove it from the bowl and transfer to a lightly floured work surface. Then, cut it into ⅓cup-sized pieces (110 g-sized). Roll those pieces into balls and, using a rolling pin, roll each one out into a flat circle with an 8 inch (20.5 cm) diameter.
4. Lightly poke holes in each dough circle using a fork then, in a very lightly greased pan, sear on both sides over low heat.
5. Set pitas aside to cool completely then store in a sealed plastic bag.

Sambal Aioli

1. Add all aioli ingredients into a food processor and pulse until well combined, set aside for assembly.

Filling & Assembly

1. In a small bowl, mix salt, pepper, and extra virgin olive extra virgin olive oil together. Then rub this mixture over the tuna. Pan sear or grill the tuna on high heat (allow the pan/grill to get very hot before putting the tuna onto it) just to mark both sides. Slice the tuna crosswise into 2-inch-thick pieces, set aside.
2. For the slaw: Finely chop the lettuce, then julienne the fire roasted pepper. Shave the red onion using a mandolin. If you do not own a mandolin, then thinly slice the onion instead.
3. Using the ingredients prepped in Step 2, make the slaw in a separate bowl. Into the bowl, add about ½ cup of the chopped lettuce, 4 slices fire roasted pepper, 1 tbsp sliced red onion. Then, add 1 tbsp sambal aioli and 2 dashes of paprika. Toss together until thoroughly combined.
4. One at a time, warm the pita bread on a clean skillet over medium heat or a grill. Be sure not to toast the bread here.
5. Once warm or (if on grill) marked, remove the pita from the skillet, open it up and put the slaw and filling inside.
6. Wrap up the pita with parchment paper (see photo). Serve and enjoy by itself or with a side of french fries.

Shrimp Saganaki

4 Servings

INGREDIENTS

20 Medium-Large Shrimps (size 36/40)

1 Tomato

1 cup Canned Tomato Purée (237mL)

½ cup Sweet Fennel (43.5g)

⅓ cup Ouzo (79mL)

¼ cup White Wine (59mL)

Salt, to taste

Black Pepper, to taste

3.5 oz Feta Cheese (100g)

1 tbsp Garlic

2 tbsp Butter

2 tbsp Extra Virgin Olive Oil

PREPARATION

1. In a large oven-safe saucepan, add extra virgin olive oil, garlic, shaved fennel, and shrimps over medium-high heat. Then, add salt, pepper, and ouzo. Flambé the ouzo by using a kitchen lighter and let the flame go out on its own.

2. Allow the sauce to reduce by half. Then, add the white wine and allow the sauce to reduce by half again.

3. Roughly dice a fresh tomato and add to the pan, then add tomato sauce to the pan and allow the sauce to reduce by half.

4. Add the butter and allow it to melt. Once melted, crumble feta cheese over the saucepan and broil on High for 5-7 minutes.

5. Serve the Shrimp Saganaki with bread. Enjoy!

Sourdough Bread and Levain

2 Loaves

INGREDIENTS

Levain
for use over 7 days

14 oz Unbleached All Purpose Flour (397g)

14 oz Whole Wheat White Flour (397g)

28 fl oz Lukewarm Water (1.59L)

Sourdough Bread

31.7 oz Unbleached All Purpose Flour (900g)

3.5 oz White Whole Wheat Flour (100g)

7 oz Levain (200g)

26.5 fl oz Lukewarm Water (750mL)

0.7 oz Salt (20g)

Baking your own sourdough can be intimidating, but luckily this dough requires zero kneading! All ingredients for this recipe are measured by weight (except water), so ***you will need*** *a scale as well as two baton baskets (as pictured in figure 9 on the next page) for proofing your sourdough loaves.*

PREPARATION

Levain

1. Combine 2 oz unbleached all purpose flour, 2 oz whole wheat white flour, and 4 oz lukewarm water in a mason jar.
2. Seal the mason jar tightly, and leave at room temperature for 24 hours.
3. The next day, discard most of this mixture, leaving only about 3.5 oz (100 g) at the bottom of the jar.
4. In a small mixing bowl, combine another 2 oz unbleached all purpose flour, 2 oz whole wheat white flour, and 4 oz lukewarm water. Once combined, add into the same jar.
5. Repeat steps 2-4 for 6 more days to grow a mature levain.

Please turn over for sourdough recipe...

Sourdough

1. Combine flours in a large bowl. In a separate bowl, dissolve the levain into 2 fl oz water, then combine with flour mixture and the rest of the water. Be sure not to overmix!

2. Cover with plastic wrap and set aside to rise for two hours at room temperature. It will double in size and have a much softer texture than before.

3. Remove the plastic wrap from the bowl. Salt the dough and, with wet hands, begin to pull the sides of the dough outward and back over itself (see photo). Repeat this for a few minutes, turning the dough between each pull and doing your best not to rip it. Cover the bowl with plastic wrap again and leave for 30 minutes.

4. Return to the dough and repeat step three 3 more times.

5. After letting the dough rest for a final 30 minutes, remove it from its bowl and transfer to a lightly floured work surface. Cut the dough in half and start rolling the dough and folding it over itself repeatedly to form a nicely rounded dough.

   NOTE *Do not knead the dough.*

6. Now, prep 2 baton baskets by coating well with flour, set aside for a moment. Pick up one of the round dough balls you just formed and flip upside down, fold the bottom 3 times. Then, place the dough, fold-side down, into the baton basket (*see figure 9*).

7. Cover both baskets firmly with plastic wrap and refrigerate for exactly 12 hours.

8. 11 hours later, preheat the oven to 500°F (260°C) with a 14-inch cast iron bread pan (7-inch depth) and its cover preheating inside as well. If you would like to bake both breads, then preheat two cast irons inside the oven.

9. After one hour of preheating, remove the cast iron bread pan from the oven. Take the dough out of the fridge, and transfer to the hot cast iron pan.

10. Cover the pan and bake for exactly 20 minutes. Then, remove the pan's lid and lower the oven temperature to 450°F (232°C) and bake for another 20 minutes.

11. Take the bread pan out of the oven, allow it to cool, and enjoy!

Figure 9 - Step 6

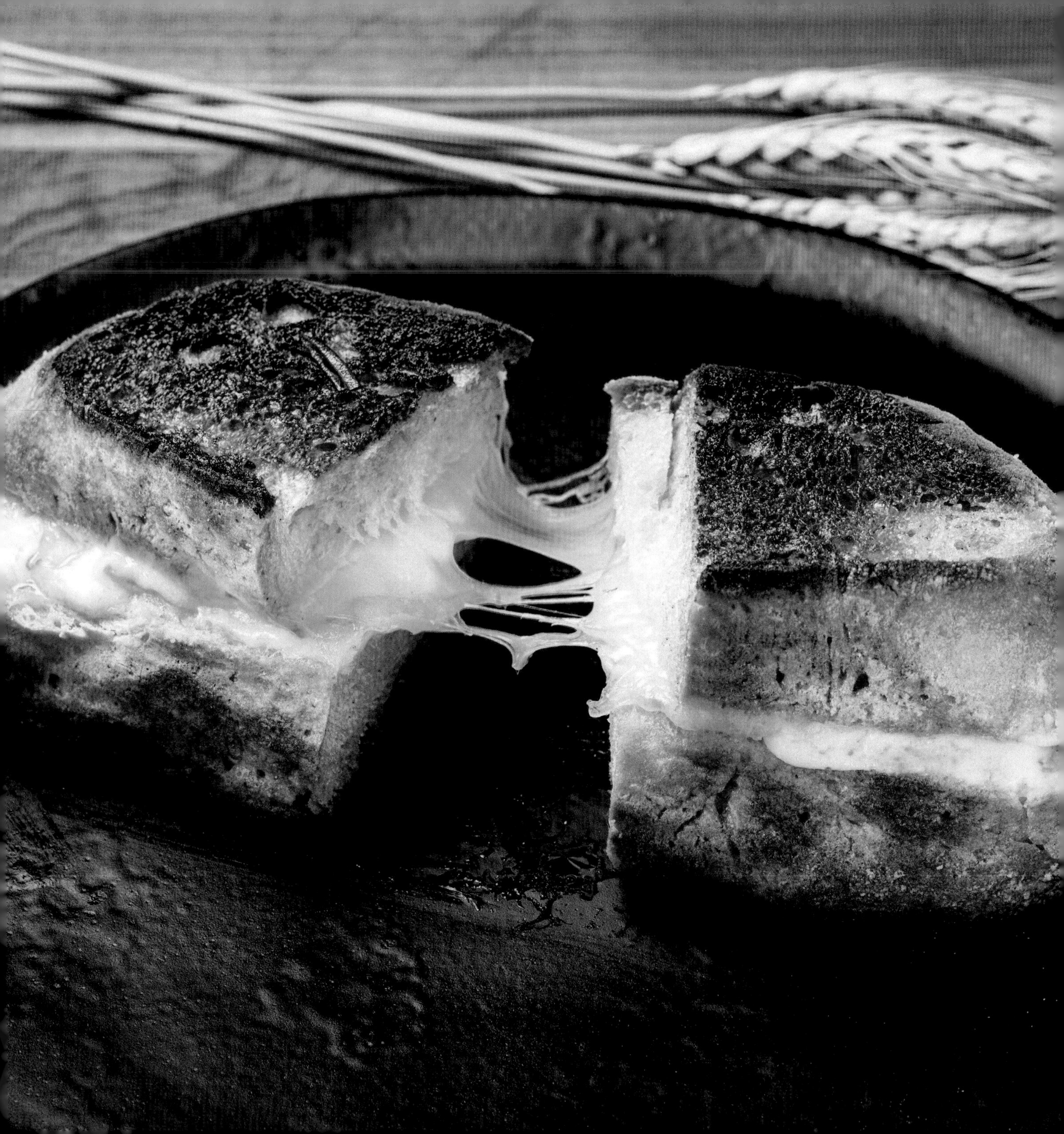

Grilled Cheese on Sourdough Bread

4 Servings

INGREDIENTS

½ lb Kefalograviera Cheese (227g)

1 sprig Fresh Thyme

1 sprig Fresh Rosemary

4 tbsp Extra Virgin Olive Oil

PREPARATION

1. Discard rosemary and thyme stems and set their leaves aside. Thinly slice the kefalograviera cheese and set aside for assembly.

2. Cut the bread into 8 thick slices, about 2 inches thick.

3. In a cast iron skillet, add the extra virgin olive oil and set over medium heat. Place rosemary and thyme into the skillet and add one slice of sourdough.

4. Top the sourdough with 2-3 slices of kefalograviera cheese and cover with another slice of bread. When the bottom slice is golden brown, flip the sandwich and cook until both sides are golden brown and cheese is melted.

5. Repeat 3 more times until you have 4 sandwiches. Enjoy!

Seafood Moussaka

4 Servings

INGREDIENTS

Seafood Mixture

1 Large Garlic Clove
2 tbsp Extra Virgin Olive Oil, plus more
⅓ cup White Wine (80mL)
10 Jumbo Shrimps (size 36/40)
20 Mussels
6 Scallops, cut in half
1 tbsp Butter

Tomato Béchamel

7 tbsp Butter (100g)
1 cup Flour (100g)
1 tsp Nutmeg
2 Eggs
½ cup Parmesan (45g)
4 cups Milk (1L)
2 tbsp Double Concentrated Tomato Paste

Roasted Vegetables

4 Medium Eggplants
4 Large Potatoes
Extra Virgin Olive Oil, to taste
Salt, to taste
Black Pepper, to taste

Assembly

3 tbsp Kefalograviera Cheese

PREPARATION

Seafood Mixture

1. Set a large saucepan over medium-high heat. Add extra virgin olive oil, garlic, scallops, shrimp, and mussels.
2. Next, add the white wine and flambé using a kitchen lighter. Allow the flame to go out on its own, then add tomato sauce and reduce by half.
3. Add the butter, allow to melt and stir to incorporate. Set this mixture aside for assembly.

Tomato Béchamel

NOTE *Make sure to allow milk to come up to room temperature before making your roux.*

1. **Make a roux** Melt the butter in a medium saucepan, then add the flour and stir together until well incorporated.
2. Give the flour a moment to cook while gently stirring, then add the milk one cup at a time, stirring constantly. Add nutmeg and keep stirring until the béchamel is thick and coats the back of a spoon.
3. Once the béchamel texture is achieved, whisk in tomato paste until well combined.
4. About 30 seconds later, transfer tomato béchamel to a heat safe mixing bowl. Add eggs to the mixture and whisk well.
5. Lastly, gradually add parmesan and continue whisking until incorporated. Cover, and set aside.

Roasted Vegetables & Assembly

1. Preheat the oven to 375°F (190°C).
2. Cut the potatoes and eggplants crosswise into 2-inch-thick slices. Spread them out onto a baking sheet with extra virgin olive oil, salt, and pepper. Bake until soft (usually up to 30 minutes).

TIP *Check for readiness by poking your potato/eggplant with a fork. If the fork pierces it easily, then it's ready.*

3. Once potatoes and eggplant have softened, remove from the oven and set aside. Change oven temperature to 400°F (200°C).
4. Form an even layer of eggplant in the bottom of a large, deep baking pan (cast iron pan recommended). Next, add a layer of the potatoes on top of the eggplant. Lastly, add the seafood mixture and top with béchamel then kefalograviera.
5. Bake for 25-30 minutes and serve. Enjoy!

Couscous Stuffed Calamari with Ladolemono Sauce

4 Servings

INGREDIENTS

Ladolemono

7 fl oz Fresh Lemon Juice (200mL)
2.5 cups Extra Virgin Olive Oil (600mL)
1 tsp Salt
1 dash of Saffron
1 tsp Dried Ground Mustard

Stuffed Calamari

4 pieces Large, Whole Calamari (size U5)
2 cups Couscous (346g)
2 tbsp Parsley
2 tbsp Mint
2 tbsp Dill
½ tbsp Sweet Fennel
1 Carrot
2 Garlic Cloves
3 tbsp Tomato Paste
Salt, to taste
Black Pepper, to taste
1 tbsp Extra Virgin Olive Oil

Squid tubes, otherwise known as calamari, are a common delicacy on Kythira. Pairing them with the refreshing couscous and veggie stuffing is my favorite way to eat them. This recipe calls for 4 whole large (U5-sized) squid tubes. If you do not want to use this size, then you can use 12 pieces of smaller squid tubes.

PREPARATION

Ladolemono

1. Add all ingredients together in a mason jar and seal, then shake for at least one minute, until fully combined.

NOTE *You may keep this sauce sealed at room temperature for up to 10 days. Always be sure to shake well before use.*

Stuffed Calamari

1. Finely chop the parsley, mint, dill, and fennel. Then, dice the carrot and mince the cloves of garlic. Set aside.
2. Boil couscous for 12 minutes until softened, then drain and transfer to a bowl with the prepared vegetables. Mix thoroughly to combine.
3. Carefully stuff each piece of calamari with a spoon until almost filled. Then, use a toothpick to close up the opening so the stuffing doesn't fall out as they cook.
4. Grill them over charcoal for 4 minutes on each side and serve with ladolemono. Enjoy!

Orzo Seafood Youvetsi

4-6 Servings

INGREDIENTS

Seafood

20 Mussels
6 Large Scallops (size U10)
10 Jumbo Shrimps (size 36/40)
10 Clams (Manila recommended)
1 tbsp Extra Virgin Olive Oil

Orzo

2 cups Orzo Pasta (200g)
2 Garlic Cloves
2 tbsp Tomato Paste
1 cup Canned Tomato Purée (237mL)
1 cup Fresh Tomato (200g)
¼ cup Ouzo (59mL)
⅓ cup White Wine (79mL)
3 tbsp Butter (60g)
½ of a Sweet Fennel Stalk
2 oz Feta (50g)

PREPARATION

Seafood

1. Set a large pot with water (about 1-inch deep) over high heat. Set a steam basket in the pot and wait for the water to boil.

2. Place all seafood into the steam basket. Cover and steam for 7 minutes and discard shells.

NOTE *As you can see in the recipe photo, I did not discard all the seafood shells because they are beautiful for plating purposes. If you would like to do the same, keep a few shelled mussels/clams/shrimp to the side for plating.*

3. Lightly pan sear the steamed seafood with 1 tbsp extra virgin olive oil, and salt and pepper, to taste.

Orzo

1. Dice tomato(s), set aside. Boil water in a medium pot in preparation for the orzo pasta. Be sure to salt the water. Add orzo into boiling water and cook until al dente.

2. Meanwhile in an oven-safe saucepan, add the minced garlic and shaved fennel and sauté, about 2 minutes.

3. Add ouzo and flambé using a kitchen lighter. Allow the flame to go out on its own so the alcohol can cook off, then add white wine and allow to cook for a couple minutes to cook off as welll.

4. Add the tomato paste, tomato purée, and diced tomatoes to the pan and season with salt and pepper to taste. Remove from heat.

5 Next, add the cooked orzo and the seafood into the pan and stir to combine. Crumble feta over top and broil on high for approximately 15 minutes. Serve and enjoy!

Goat Cheese Gnocchi

4-6 Servings

INGREDIENTS

Gnocchi

31.7 Of Goat Cheese (900g)
1 ½ cup All Purpose Flour (192g)
1 Egg
1 ½ tbsp Extra Virgin Olive Oil
½ tsp Black Pepper
½ cup Parmesan (45g)

Figure 10 - Step 3

Aji Amarillo Beurre Blanc

2 Shallots
3 ½ Sticks Unsalted Butter (400g)
½ cup Heavy Cream (118mL)
1 tbsp Salt, plus more
1 ½ tbsp Aji Amarillo Paste
4 tbsp White Wine (nothing too sweet)

In Greece, we have our own version of gnocchi, called "gogizes" or "gogges," depending what region you're from. This is my goat cheese variation of the dish dressed with an aji amarillo beurre blanc sauce. Aji amarillo is a Peruvian yellow pepper with a hefty kick and some sweetness to it.

PREPARATION

Gnocchi

1. In a bowl, mix together the dry ingredients (flour, black pepper, shaved parmesan), then in another bowl mix together the wet ingredients (goat cheese, egg, extra virgin olive oil).
2. Incorporate wet ingredients into the bowl of dry ingredients until a smooth and firm dough forms.

TIP *It is best to work with the goat cheese at refrigerator temp, so leave it in the fridge until you need it!*

3. Cut the dough into 6 equal pieces. Roll each piece by hand into a rope-like shape until the dough is about a half-inch thick (or 1.5 cm). Using oblique (slanted) cuts, cut each rope into 3/4-inch-long pieces (2 cm). *See figure 10 to the left.*

TIP *If this recipe yields more gnocchi dough than needed, you may store them in an airtight container in the freezer for up to 3-4 months.*

4. Bring well-salted water to a boil on the stove. Drop gnocchi dough pieces into boiling water. Keep your eye on the pot because once the gnocchi surface, they're ready!

Aji Amarillo Beurre Blanc

1. Finely chop shallots. Set a large non-stick saucepan over medium heat, add shallots and salt to the pan. The salt helps with the dehydration and caramelization of the shallots without using butter or oil.
2. Once the shallots are golden in color and caramelized, add white wine to the pan and reduce to less than half. Please note that you should be using medium heat so that sauce does not come to a boil at any point.
3. Begin adding butter in small increments until fully melted and well-incorporated. Once the butter is melted (but not boiling), add in 1 tbsp salt, aji amarillo paste, and heavy cream. Simmer for about 5-7 minutes, until reduced and thickened.
4. Serve the desired amount of sauce with about 20 gnocchis per serving and enjoy!

Leftover Instructions

This sauce can be refrigerated for up to 5 days if it is covered well with plastic wrap to prevent a skin from forming overtop. When pulled from the fridge, the sauce will have thickened more and will need extra care. Add 4 tbsp of sauce to the saucepan with an extra ⅓ cup (79mL) of heavy cream and reduce until thickened, then add approximately 20 pieces of gnocchi. Serve and enjoy!

During the winter months, my friends and I made a habit of meeting up at the Kapsali Bay Harbor, late at night, with a 500m (1640 ft) fishing net. Because the net was so large, we would tie one end of it to the posts at the end of the harbor and split up. Two of us would remain at the harbor while the other two would bring the opposite end of the net to the beach, overlooking the same bay. The net was so massive that we could only pull it taught from the far end of the harbor to the middle of the beach at least! It could catch anything; from fish, to clams, to squid.

For the next few hours, we would use flashlights, signaling to each other from across the bay for when to pull and release the net. Once we caught more than enough fish to feed the whole island! Once we had caught our fill, we would reconvene on the beach to set up a bonfire to grill our night's catch to perfection. We would spend the rest of our starlit hours grilling fish and squid over the fire, pairing them with fries and salad, and using large rocks found nearby as plates. Primed with full bellies, ouzo, and laughter, we would stay on the beach until sunrise. The flavors in this dish remind me of those many happy nights spent at Kapsali Bay, and I hope you'll be able to taste them too.

This recipe uses the en papillote method to bake the fish to perfection. This method consists of placing the fish and other ingredients on parchment paper which is then folded upwards around the edges to keep all juices and flavors packed in with the fish as it cooks.

Perka in Paper

2 Servings

INGREDIENTS

1 lb Perch Fillet, skin on (450g)
1 Carrot
1 Zucchini
½ Sweet Fennel
4 Cherry Tomatoes
Salt, to taste
Black Pepper, to taste
1 cup White Wine (237mL)
2 tbsp Butter
1 Clove Garlic
3 tbsp Extra Virgin Olive Oil

PREPARATION

1. Preheat oven to 450°F (230°C).
2. Julienne the carrot and zucchini, and add to sauté pan with minced garlic, shaved fennel, and 1 tbsp extra virgin olive oil over medium-high heat.
3. Sauté until vegetables begin to soften, then add white wine and flambé using a kitchen lighter. Allow the liquid in the pan to reduce by half. Next, add butter, remove from heat, and set aside.
4. Set a skillet over medium-high heat and add 2 tbsp extra virgin olive oil. Once the skillet is hot, add the perch fillet skin-side down and sear until the skin is crispy. Remove from heat and set aside.
5. Set down a sheet of parchment paper and transfer the contents of the sautéed veggie pan over the center of the parchment. Top with the perch fillet and add cherry tomatoes. Fold both sides of the parchment paper and turn the two ends like a candy wrapper (*see recipe photo*).
6. Place the filled parchment paper into a baking pan and cover with another similarly sized pan. Bake for 15-20 minutes and serve. Enjoy!

DESSERTS

One of my favorite desserts to get in New York City is the cannoli. I've always loved getting them to-go at my local bakery and impatiently pulling them out of the box right as I leave the shop. I love the experience of biting into them, with the loud crunch of the dough as the soft cream escapes from the opposite end. Desserts should be indulgent and fun, and the cannoli is just that. A few years ago, I wanted to create a new Greek dessert for my restaurant's menu; my mind was immediately drawn to the cannoli.

I decided to start experimenting with kataifi dough and, soon enough, I created the Kataifi Cigar by wrapping kataifi around cannoli molds to form the hollow cigar shape. Once the cigars were baked to golden perfection, I filled them with my favorite kind of cream filling: diplomat cream, which is made by mixing a custard with whipped cream.

When I put the Kataifi Cigar on my restaurant's dessert menu, I received a lot of very positive feedback. Patrons would rave about them to me, asking for my recipe. Eventually, I started getting calls from local Greek market owners saying that people kept showing up at their shop looking for the dessert they had tried at my restaurant. The owners would ask if they could have my recipe so that they could sell it! Of course, a great chef never reveals their secret recipes, but the praise and rising demand for this dessert astonished me so much that I have finally decided to present it to the world here. I hope you love it as much as I do!

Kataifi is a form of phyllo dough that is shredded into many long, hair-like strands and used in many different Greek foods, both sweet and savory. This recipe has quite a few moving parts, but it is well worth the effort, I promise! **You will need 6 cannoli molds which are about 6-inches in length and have a 1-inch diameter.**

Kataifi Cigar

6 Cigars

INGREDIENTS

Diplomat Cream

4 cups Whole Milk (1L)
1 Tahitian Vanilla Bean
1 cup Sugar (200g)
¾ cup + 2 tsp Corn Flour (110g)
4 Whole Eggs
1 Egg Yolk
6 cups Whipped Cream (250g)

Whipped Cream

4 cups Heavy Cream (1L)
1 ½ cup Powdered Sugar (172g)
1 Tahitian Vanilla Bean

Kataifi Cigars

2 lb Kataifi Phyllo Dough (900g)
2 lb Butter (900g)
1 tbsp Sesame Seeds
1 tbsp Poppy Seeds
6 cups Simple Syrup (1.4L)

PREPARATION

Diplomat Cream & Whipped Cream Garnish

NOTE *I recommend making the custard filling one day in advance so that it can set overnight in the refrigerator.*

Day 1
Let's make the custard.

1. Whisk milk, sugar, and vanilla bean insides together in a saucepan. Bring this mixture to a boil.
2. In another bowl, whisk together the sugar, the corn flour, and the eggs. Once well incorporated, pour a small amount of the boiling mixture into the eggs to prevent the eggs from curdling. Then, pour that mixture back into the boiling milk mixture and mix thoroughly. Once thickened, remove from heat and pour into a tray.
3. Cover this with plastic wrap and refrigerate your custard overnight.

Day 2
Let's make the whipped cream. Part of it will be mixed with the custard to make diplomat cream while the rest will be used as garnish for your cigars.
I recommend doing this while the cigars are baking.

4. Add heavy cream into a stand mixer (whisk attachment) and turn on high. Slowly add sugar, then the vanilla bean insides. Whisk until soft peaks form.
5. Take the custard out of the refrigerator and transfer into a large bowl and mix for one minute to soften (preferably with a stand mixer or electric whisk). Then, slowly fold in 6 cups (250g) of the whipped cream to create your diplomat cream filling. Set aside.

Cigars & Assembly

1. Remove kataifi dough from packaging and allow it to come to room temperature, about two hours. Be sure to cover it with a damp kitchen towel to prevent the dough from drying.

2. In the meantime, make the simple syrup as per the instructions on the next page.

3. Once the kataifi reaches room temperature, preheat convection oven to 325°F (163°C). Melt the butter and set aside.

4. Set down about 30-40 strands of phyllo dough onto your work surface and butter them generously using a pastry brush. Sprinkle with desired amount of sesame and poppy seeds.

5. Wrap the pipe tightly with the buttered and seeded phyllo strands, starting on one end and moving toward the other.

TIP *Try not to wrap the dough around the pipe by hand as it will become very messy and inconsistent. The best way to do this is to place the dough strands on your work surface and attach one end of the dough to the pipe. Then, roll the pipe over the dough carefully it until the dough is completely wrapped around the pipe from one end to the other.*

6. Once the pipe is fully covered, place it onto a silicone baking sheet. Continue to do this until all the dough is wrapped around pipes so that the metal is no longer visible.

7. Bake for about 10-17 minutes until golden brown. Remove from the oven and place onto a perforated sheet rack over a sheet pan. Once set on the rack, generously drizzle room temperature simple syrup over the kataifi cigars, allowing the excess to drop down onto the baking sheet below the rack.

8. Allow them to cool and set into their shape for 5 minutes. Then, using tweezers, carefully pull the metal pipe out from inside the kataifi cigars.

9. Transfer diplomat cream filling into piping bags and fill each cigar generously. Garnish with leftover whipped cream and serve. Enjoy!

TIP *You may also add a shaped metal piping tip to your bag to give a nice shape to the garnish.*

Simple Syrup

6 cup yield

INGREDIENTS

5 cups Sugar (1kg)
3 cups Water (710mL)
1 Cinnamon Stick
2 Cloves

Variation for Bergamot Sponge Cake

15 cups Sugar (3kg)
9 cups Water (2.1L)
3 Cinnamon Sticks
6 Cloves
5-6 Bergamots (skin/peel only)

Variation for Baklava with Corfu Butter

20 cups Sugar (4kg)
12 cups Water (2.85L)
4 Cinnamon Sticks
8 Cloves

PREPARATION

1. Put all syrup ingredients into a small saucepan, stir, and bring to a boil. Let this boil for two or three minutes. Any longer and the syrup will begin to crystalize and take on a crunchy texture; this is not what you want.

2. Remove the syrup from the hot saucepan and set aside to cool.

3. Once cooled, strain out solids and store in an airtight jar in the fridge for up to 10 days.

Note For the Bergamot Sponge Cake Variation *Try to leave out as much of the bergamot pith (white part between skin and fruit) as you can since it is very bitter.*

Bergamot Sponge Cake

12 Servings

INGREDIENTS

Orange Peel Confit

8-9 Oranges

Bergamot Sponge

6 eggs

2 cups Milk (475mL)

2 cups Vegetable Oil (475mL)

2 cups Sugar (400g)

3 tbsp Baking Powder

½ tsp Baking Soda

5 pieces of #7 Phyllo Dough

Seasonal; bergamots, a notoriously sour and fragrant citrus fruit, are only freshly available in the summer. There is no bergamot in the sponge because it would make for a very bitter one, but its flavors are perfectly mixed into the simple syrup used to soak the sponge.

PREPARATION

NOTE *Two days ahead of baking the sponge, set out 5 pieces of #7 phyllo dough uncovered at room temperature. This will allow the dough to dry out completely for when it goes into the batter.*

Orange Peel Confit

1. Place 8-9 whole oranges into a large pot and cover with cold water.
2. Set over high heat and leave the oranges to come to a boil.
3. Allow to boil for one hour, then put oranges in a cool bath (ice water) to stop the cooking process. Peel oranges and discard (or eat!) the fruit. Set aside the orange peels.

Bergamot Simple Syrup

NOTE *Please refer to page 91 for the instructions and ingredients for the bergamot simple syrup.*

Bergamot Sponge

1. Preheat oven to 325°F and grease a baking tray with butter, set aside.
2. In a food processor, beat the eggs and sugar until light and fluffy. Continuing to beat the mixture, slowly add in half of the orange peels. Then add baking soda and baking powder. Add the milk. Then, add the rest of the orange peels.
3. While the food processor is still running, add vegetable oil slowly in a continuous stream, allowing it to emulsify into the mixture.
4. Once incorporated, pour the batter into a greased baking tray (24x15 inch) and set aside for a moment. Next, break apart the dried out phyllo dough into many small pieces. Then, bit by bit, fully submerge the phyllo bits into the batter. Try to evenly disperse the bits throughout the batter. This helps with the structural integrity of this already very moist sponge.
5. Bake for 25 minutes. Once the sponge comes out of the oven, pour room temperature syrup over the sponge. Serve and enjoy!

NOTE *The syrup must be room temperature or colder when poured over the hot sponge. If it is too hot, it will change the texture of the cake.*

Baklava with Corfu Butter

12-18 Servings

INGREDIENTS

2 Packs of Phyllo Dough #7

1 lb Ground Walnuts (450g)

1 ½ tsp Cinnamon

2 lb melted, Clarified Butter (900g)

⅔ cups Corfu Butter (150g)

⅔ cups Unsalted Butter (150g)

Simple Syrup (See page 91)

PREPARATION

1. Allow 2 packs of phyllo dough to defrost overnight in a refrigerator.
2. Please refer to the Baklava Variation of the Simple Syrup recipe on page 91 at this stage of preparation.
3. Preheat oven to 325°F (160°C). Grease a baking sheet with butter. Then, carefully open the pack and unfold the phyllo, placing each layer on a greased baking sheet as is. Do this until you finish one pack.
   NOTE *It's okay if phyllo dough sheets rip as you place them down, just try to keep their form intact as best as you can throughout the process!*
4. Add ground walnuts and cinnamon into a medium mixing bowl, stir together until combined. Then, top the phyllo dough pile with this mixture, completely covering the dough sheet.
5. Open the second pack of phyllo dough. Carefully unfold and add one sheet of phyllo dough on top of walnut mixture. Generously brush melted butter over the single sheet. Repeat this process until the second pack of dough is completely used up.
6. Using the pastry brush, press down on the edges of the dough to seal it. Cut the dough into diamond-shaped pieces (as pictured).
7. Melt and combine corfu with unsalted clarified butter then pour over baklava. Once absorbed into baklava, bake for 50 minutes.
8. Take out of the oven and immediately pour (room temperature or colder) simple syrup over the whole sheet of baklava.
9. Allow to cool for twenty minutes and serve. Enjoy!

Honey Cheesecake from Santorini

12 Servings

INGREDIENTS

Biscuit Crust

9 oz Biscuits (250g)

7 tbsp Butter, melted (100g)

Softened Butter, as needed

Cheesecake

3.3 lbs Manouri Cheese (1.5kg)

1 ½ cup Honey, plus more (355mL)

½ cup Superfine Sugar (115g)

6 Whole Eggs

2 tsp Vanilla Extract

1 tsp Cinnamon, garnish

PREPARATION

Biscuit Crust

1. Using softened butter, grease the sides and bottom of a 12" diameter springform pan. Set aside.

__NOTE__ I highly recommend that if you are looking to buy a new springform pan for this recipe, that you choose to buy one made with stainless steel as these hold up wonderfully over time.

2. Take 9 oz of your preferred biscuits and put them into a food processor. For example, this amounts to 16 sheets of graham crackers. Pulse until the biscuits are ground up (you may choose to grind them up very finely or more coarsely).

3. Add the melted butter into the food processor and pulse just until combined with the crumbs. Transfer this into the greased springform pan and compress it down to evenly cover the pan's base.

4. Refrigerate the pan containing the biscuit crust for at least 1 hour.

Cheesecake

1. Meanwhile, preheat oven to 375°F (190°C). Crumble manouri cheese and set aside.

2. Using a stand mixer, mix together honey and sugar until fluffy. Then, add crumbled cheese and beat the mixture again until incorporated.

3. While the mixer is still running, add one egg at a time, waiting for each egg to be fully incorporated before adding the next. Once the batter reaches a creamy texture, add in the vanilla extract and mix just until combined.

4. Pour the batter into the greased pan and bake for 40 minutes.

5. Once baked through, allow the cheesecake to cool completely and remove the spring form from the base of the pan to reveal your beautiful cheesecake. Serve cold with honey and cinnamon on top. Enjoy!

DIETARY INDEX

Gluten-Free

Vegetarian

Pescatarian

Vegan

ACKNOWLEDGEMENTS

I would like to thank **Athena M. Villard** from Villanelle Press for meticulously editing and managing this cookbook project from start to finish. Thank you for going above and beyond with this cookbook and teaming up with me.
Please find more information about Athena M. Villard at
www.athenavillard.com

•

I would like to thank **Nathan Luckhurst** from Villanelle Press for diligently editing, proofreading, and consulting on this project.

•

I would like to thank **Ilir Rizaj** for having been the best photographer anyone could ask for. Thank you for donating your time, your efforts, and your expertise.
Please find more information about Ilir Rizaj, Photographer here:
www.ilirrizaj.com

•

I would like to thank everybody at **1760 Homestead Farm** in Northville, New York. Thank you all for lending me your beautiful kitchen and fire pit to use for all the recipe images in this book. I would also like to thank you all for planting and cultivating my Kythirian vlita seeds so that I may eat and cook with the same vlita plant I've had since I was a child.
Please find more information about 1760 Homestead Farm on instagram
@1760_homestead_farm

•

I would like to thank **Kiki Truffles** for donating the beautiful Greek truffles seen on the book's cover.
Please find more information about Kiki Truffles at
www.kikitruffles.com

•

Last, but most certainly not least, I would like to thank a dear friend of mine, **Chef Jean-Christophe Villard**, 1998's 5-Star Diamond Award Winner. Jean-Christophe is by far one of the leading French steakhouse chefs to set foot in New York. A decade ago at Kellari Taverna you helped steer me in the right direction toward success and took me under your wing. I will never forget those days and all the guidance you gave me as my "New York Mentor".
Chef Jean-Christophe Villard has a beautiful brasserie in Paris, France, called "Au Petit Tonneau" Levallois-Perret.
Please find more information about "Au Petit Tonneau" at
www.AuPetitTonneauLevallois.com

THANK YOU!